How to make a Will?

by

Sandeep Bhalla

PREFACE

This is a legal guide written in accordance with Indian Law but it may generally be correct for all countries following Anglo-Saxon laws. Further, succession to immovable properties situated in India, shall be regulated by Indian Laws, irrespective of the domicile of such person. In other words, foreigners who own immovable assets in India, shall have to confirm to Indian Laws to make a legally competent and operative Will. This book is intended to act only as a brief introduction to the laws relating to Wills and is not intended to replace legal advice from a competent practitioner of law.

This book is intended to remove doubts and myths about Wills which are compounded by free misinformation available on the internet either as a web page or guide-lines in pdf format.

The target readers are law students and amateur beginners who wish to draft their own Will. It is however strongly advised that after drafting a Will in accordance with this book, do consult a Lawyer of your choice and get it vetted from him/her.

Caution: This book is generally applicable to Hindus, Sikh, Jain etc. domiciled in India. Most part of this Book may not be applicable to Indian Christians, Muslims and Parsees who are governed by separate customary law. It also do not apply to army-men, airmen and marines who are entitled to execute privileged Wills.

NOTES

Table of Contents

What is a Will

Will is a legal declaration of the testator/testatrix with respect to his/her property which he/she desires to be carried into effect after his death.[1]

It may be clarified that testator and testatrix are male or female (as the case may be) persons who are executing the Will. In other words a person executing a Will is called testator or testatrix, depending upon the gender.

In simple terms Will is an ambulatory document which takes effect only after the death of it's executant and result in transmission of property to the persons named in the Will. These persons who inherit the property are called legatees.

Thus the three most important requirements of the Will are:

> 1. It should contain clear and specific directions for disposal or transmission of property to specific persons or institutions
>
> 2. It should be effective only after the death of testator.
>
> 3. It should be revocable during the life time of testator.

There is no restriction upon number of Wills. A person is free to execute a fresh Will, which may be in entirely different from the terms of previous Will. It is only the last Will that shall be treated as effect Will in law. How ever it is advisable that each Will may mention the details of previous Wills and expressly supersede its terms to avoid confusion.

---

1   See section 2 (h) of Succession Act, 1925.

History about origin of Wills

(Impatient may skip to next chapter)

Law of Wills is the most ancient law, prevalent from the time of Romans. The origin of the will can be referred to ancient times as it is shown to be in existence as in Babylon and Assyria. It was considered that the idea of disposition by Will was the gift of Rome's expiring civilisation to Rome's rude conquerors, awakened at last, by closer contact with the civilization to a better life the laws prevalent in various civilised countries concede to the owner of the property the right of determining by Will to whom he effects which he leaves behind him shall pass. Such a right is, however, subject to statutory laws.[2]

Roman law has vastly influenced the present day English law of succession. During Roman period Will (called as Testamentum) could also be effectual during the lifetime of the person who made it. The person making the Will must have *locus curtius* (or the earnest to make) Will. Initially it could also be made in public *vivâ voce* (i.e. Orally). The testator had to declare his will in the presence of seven witnesses; and it could not be changed. These Oral Wills were called *nuncupative* testaments. However the danger involved in trusting the will of the dead to the memory of the living soon abolished these; and all testaments were ordered to be in writing. During Roman period the whole property of the testator could not be alienated. The rights of heirs and descendants were protected by enactment which secured to them a legal minimum, the *querela inofficiosi testamenti* being the remedy of those passed over. The age at which testamentary

---

2   Bhagya Wati v. General Public, AIR 1995 P&H 201.

capacity began was fourteen in the case of males, twelve in the case of females. Women originally had no *testamentifactio* (or testamentary capacity), and when they did acquire the power, they could only exercise it with the *auctoritas* of a Tutor. Of course a daughter in the power of her father, whether she was married or unmarried, and a wife in *manu* could never make a will. The rules therefore as to a woman's capacity to make a will, could apply only to unmarried women after the death of their father and to widows who were not in the power of a father. Slaves had no had no *testamentifactio* (or testamentary capacity) to make Will.

Indian law relating to testamentary succession was governed by different laws for different classes of citizens on the basis of religion. Indian Christians, Muslims and Parsees are still governed by different laws. Hindus which were governed by Mitakshara and Dayalbhaga branches of Hindu Laws are now governed by statutory laws of succession which are namely the Indian succession Act, 1925 and Hindu Succession Act, 1956 which is nothing but application of principles of English Laws of succession, subject to certain deviations in accordance with the circumstances.

How to make a Will

Notes

Legal terms and definitions

[3]**"Administrator"** means a person appointed by competent authority to administer the estate of a deceased person when there is no executor.

"Codicil" means an instrument made in relation to a will , and explaining, altering or adding to its dispositions, and shall be deemed to from part of the will.

"District Judge" mean the Judge of a principal Civil Court of original jurisdiction.

"Executor" mean the person to whom the execution of the last will of a deceased person is, by the testator's appointment , confided. A universal legatee or a beneficiary to whom all or most of inheritance is passed on can also be treated as an executor.

"India" means the territory of India excluding the State of Jammu and Kashmir.

"Indian Christian" means a native of India who is, or in good faith claims to be, of unmixed Asiatic decent and who professes any form of the Christian religion. Obviously a person of Anglo-Indian descent is not covered in this definition.

"Minor" means any person subject to the Indian majority Act, 1875 (9 of 1875) who has not attained his majority within the meaning of that Act, and any other person who has not completed the age of eighteen years; and "minority" means the status of any such person.

---

3   Partly defined by section 2 of Succession Act, 1925.

"**Probate**" means the copy of a will certified under the seal of court of competent jurisdiction with a grant of administration to the estate of the testator. Every legal proceedings ends in a judgement. In a suit the last operative portion of judgement is enforceable on its own and it is called a Decree. In Testamentary jurisdiction, if court accepts the Will, it grants an order along with certified copy of Will. This Order is called Probate. The Court proceedings which finally culminate into grant or refusal of Probate are called probate proceedings. Sometimes these are also called as Testamentary proceedings.

"**State**" includes any division of India having a court of the last resort. In other words it includes union territory as well because each UT, like every State has a High Court as court of last resort.

"**Will**" mean the legal declaration of the intention of a testator with respect to his property which he desires to be carried into effect after his death.

Difference between A Will & other documents

A document which purports to transfer the property *in presenti* i.e. immediately or during the life time of testator is not a Will. If transfer is in lieu of another property it is called Exchange. If transfer is immediate but for monetary consideration it is a Conveyance. A transfer without monetary consideration but out of love and affection for transferee and effective immediately is a Gift. But a Gift made in contemplation of death is dealt with differently.

A gift is said to be made in contemplation of death where a man who is ill and expects to die shortly of his illness, delivers, to another the possession of any moveable property to keep as a gift in case the donor shall die of that illness. A gift made in contemplation of death of any moveable property which he could dispose of by will, may be resumed by the giver; and shall not take effect if donor recovers from the illness during which it was made; nor if he survives the person to whom it was made.[4] This is explained by these *illustrations:*

> (i) 'A', being ill, and in expectation of death, delivers to B, to be retained by him in case of A's death,
>> a watch;
>> a bond granted by 'C' to 'A';
>> a bank-note
> a promissory note of the Central Government endorsed in blanks;
> a bill of exchange endorsed in blank'
> certain mortgage deeds.
> 'A' dies of the illness during which he delivered these articles. B is entitled to.—

---

4   Section 191 *ibid.*

the watch;
the debt secured by C's bond;
the bank-note;
the promissory note of the Central Government;
the bill of exchange; the money secured by the mortgage deeds.

(ii) 'A', being ill, and in expectation of death, delivers to 'B' the key of a trunk or the key of a warehouse in which goods of bulk belonging to 'A' are deposited, with the intention of giving him the control over the contents of the trunk or over the deposited goods and desires him to keep them in case of A's death. 'A' dies of the illness during which he delivered these articles. 'B' is entitled to the trunk and its contents or to A's goods of bulk in the warehouse.

(iii) 'A' being ill, and in expectation of death, puts aside certain articles in separate parcels and marks upon the parcels respectively the names of 'B' and 'C'. The parcels are not delivered during the life of 'A', 'A' dies of the illness during which he set aside the parcels. 'B' and 'C' are not entitled to the contents of the parcels.

Therefore a Gift in contemplation of death becomes operative only in case of its actual delivery coupled with the death of donor but stands automatically revoked if donor does not die. This is different from a Will which is never automatically revoked.

Like a mortgage deed a will need not be executed and attested first before it is presented for registration. Only two safeguards are needed for a will, namely, execution and attestation. If these are supplied at the registration, the requirements are fulfilled. The case of a will therefore is entirely different from a case of a mortgage and cannot be relied upon as a clear guide.[5]

---

5   Lechman Singh v. Surendra Bahadur Singh, AIR 1932 All 527.

Why we need a Will?

Death is an interruption of enjoyment of right, title and interest in the property unless the right, title and interest is transferred to another owner. Ordinarily, if there is no Will[6], subject to customary laws, a dead person's property is distributed among his nearest legal heirs like spouse and children. If these near relatives are not there than it is transmitted upon other relatives like grand children or siblings or parents etc., failing which among the distant relatives related by blood called kindred relationships[7]. If there is no living relative at all, the properties vest in the Government which is called escheat.

The object of creating a Will is to avoid statutory transmission of property. If there is a Will, directing the manner of disposition of property after death, the terms of Will prevail upon the statutory manner of succession which operates only in case of intestate succession or absence of Will.

However where bequest is made to the "heirs" or "right heirs" or "relations" or "kindred" or "nearest of kin" of a particular person without any qualifying the terms and the class so designated forms the direct and independent object of bequest, the property bequeathed, shall be distributed as if it had belonged to such person and he hand died intestate in respect of it, leaving assets for the payment of his debts independently of such property.[8] See the following *illustrations:*

> (i) '*A*' leaves his property "to my own nearest relations". The property goes to those who would be entitled to if it '*A*' had died

6   Called 'intestate succession'.
7   See section 23 to 28 of the Succession Act, 1925.
8   Section 93 *ibid.*

intestate, leaving assets for the payment of his debts independently of such property.

(ii) *'A'* bequeaths 10,000 rupees "to *'B'* for his life, and, after the death of *'B'*, to my own right heirs". The legacy after *B*'s death belongs to those who would be entitled to it if it had formed part of *A*'s un-bequeathed property.

There is no way to ensure that a near relative shall not be entitled to any property after the death of testator, except by creating a Will. Similarly, intestate (succession by law in the absence of will) is always in favour of blood relatives. Several other relations like a friend, divorced spouse or step children get nothing unless there is a Will making them entitled. Children born out of wedlock (Bastards) get same treatment as lawful children.

The Courts make all efforts to determine the real intention of the testator by reading the Will as a whole and giving effect to the intentions of the testatorr. Construction, which would advance the intention of the testator has to be preferred and as far as possible effect is required to be given to every disposition contained in the Will, unless the law prevents such effect being given to it.[9]

---

9   Bhura vs. Kashiram, AIR 1994 SC 1202: 1994 (2) SCC 111.

Properties covered by Will.

A bequest by Will can be made in respect of self acquired properties of the testator. Ancestral properties or impartiable estates can not be the subject matter of a Will. Similarly a bequest which has effect of depriving the right of maintenance to any person, can not be made.[10]

To find out whether a property is or is not ancestral in the hands of a particular person, not merely the relationship between the original and the present holder but the mode of transmission also must be looked at and the property can ordinarily be reckoned as ancestral only if the present holder has got it by virtue of his being a son or descendant of the original owner. There is no warrant for saying that according to the Mitakshara, an affectionate gift by the father to the son constitutes ipso facto ancestral property in the hands of the donee.[11]

A licence to occupy and/or use a premises or any chattel is personal, unless terms specify otherwise. Therefore ordinarily such licence can not be bequeathed by Will.

Leasehold properties can be bequeathed by Will[12] but a tenancy protected under Rent Control Act, are statutory tenancy and therefore can not be transferred by Will.

The agreement of lease confers on the lessee the right to possess the immovable property subject matter of the lease. It being an interest in the immovable property would be covered under the expression "all my moveable and immovable properties" used in

---

10   Schedule III to Succession Act, 1925.

11   C.N. Arunachala Mudaliar vs. C.A. Muruganatha Mudaliar, AIR 1953 SC 495: 1953 SCJ 707: 1954 SCR 243.

12   Kanta Devi Agarwal vs. State of West Bengal, 2000 (1) CCC 101 Cal.

the above quoted residuary clause of the will. The word 'property' includes all legal rights of a person except his personal rights which constitute his status or personal condition.[13]

Bequest of tenancy rights in this context stands on the same footing as any other transfer by sub-lease, sale, assignment gift, volition of the tenant including un-contemplated strangers in the premises and thrusting them on the landlord, being the common element of these dispositions.[14]

The disability of a coparcener in disposing of his undivided interest in the property by Will or other testamentary document under the old Hindu Law is removed by Section 30. According to Section 4 any custom inconsistent with any provision of this enactment is abrogated. In the expression "any other law for the time being in force", the 'law' will include any statutory law or textual law or customary law. It would, therefore, follow that if there was any prohibition under the old Hindu Law the same stands removed after coming into force of Section 30 of the Hindu Succession Act.[15]

A testator can not give away all his properties by Will without making any provision for payment of his debts. The executor of a Will also can not lawfully distribute the assets of the testator to the legal heirs without first having paid all the debts.[16]

In case of a Will executed by Hindu widow in possession under a life interest, the legatee succeeds to no title. The claim of legatee is unenforceable not only against the next reversioner but also against the third person in unauthorised possession of property.[17]

---

13   Kenneth Solomon vs. Dan Singh Bawa, 1986 (1) ILR 282 Del: AIR 1986 Del 1: 1985 (28) DLT 229: 1985 (9) DRJ 292: 1985 RLR 438: 1985 (1) RCJ 679: 1986 (1) RCR 141.
14   Anant Trimbak Sabnis vs. Vasnat Partap Pandit, AIR 1980 Bom 69: 1979 Mah LJ 755.
15   Jamuna Bai vs. Surendrakumar, AIR 1995 MP 274.
16   Commissioner of Income Tax vs. Udayan Chinubhai, 1996 (5) SCC 633.
17   Shambhu Dayal vs. Pt. Basdeo Sahai, AIR 1970 All 525 (FB).

Absence of fraud or coercion & sound disposition of mind.

Will should be a voluntary act on the part of testator. A will or any part of a will, the making of which has been caused by fraud or coercion, or by such importunity which took away the free agency of the testator, is void.[18] Fraud is an act of deception which may involve misrepresentation of fact or concealment of facts.[19] See these *illustrations:*

> (i) 'A' falsely and knowingly represents to the testator that the testator's only child is dead, or that he has done some undutiful act and thereby induces the testator to make a will in his, A's favour; such will has been obtained by fraud, and is invalid.
>
> (ii) 'A', by fraud and deception, prevails upon the testator to bequeath legacy to him. The bequest is void.
>
> (iii) 'A', being a prisoner by lawful authority, makes his will. The will not invalid by reason of the imprisonment.
>
> (iv) 'A' threatens to shoot B, or to burn his house or to cause him to be arrested on a criminal charge, unless he makes a bequest in favour of 'C'. 'B', consequence, makes a bequest in favour of 'C'. The bequest is void, the making of it having been caused by coercion.
>
> (v) 'A', being of sufficient intellect, if undisturbed by the influence of other to make a will, yet being so much under the control of 'B' that he is not a free agent, makes a will, dictated by 'B'. It appears that he would not have executed the will but for fear of 'B'. The will is invalid.
>
> (vi) 'A', being in so feeble a state of health as to be unable to resist importunity, is pressed by 'B' to make a will of a certain purport and does so merely to purchase peace and in

---

18 Section 61. of Succession Act, 1925.
19 1994 (1) SCC 1.

submission to 'B'. The will is invalid.

(vii) 'A', being in such a state of health as to be capable of exercising his own judgement and volition, 'B' uses urgent intercession and persuasion with him to induce him to make a will of a certain purport. 'A', in consequence of a the intercession and persuasion, but in the free exercise of his judgement and volition, makes his will in the manner recommended by 'B'. The will is not rendered in invalid by the intercession and persuasion of 'B'.

(viii) 'A', with a view to obtaining a legacy from 'B', pays him attention and flatters him and thereby produces in him a capricious partiality to 'A'. 'B', in consequence of such attention and flattery, makes his will, by which he leaves a legacy to 'A'. The bequest is not rendered invalid by the attention and flattery of 'A'.

The testator must execute will in his sound disposition of mind[20] without any influence or coercion by any body but this does not mean that he should be in complete isolation from the beneficiaries under the Will. The Will is a solemn document which is given effect after the death of testator therefore its execution must be free from doubts about free will or the understanding of its contents by the testator.

---

20   Section 59 ibid.

What is a Codicil?

Codicil means an instrument made in relation to a Will and explaining, altering or adding to its disposition and shall be deemed to be part of the Will.

In other words codicil is a document purporting to alter, amend or explain, a prior executed Will. The amendment can be of any type. Amendment could be to correct a clerical error or to change the terms of Will by making changes in the share of legatee or the description of property or properties. There is no restriction upon the scope of Codicil. After execution of a Codicil, the Will has to read and given effect, only along with the Codicil.

Practically Codicil is not a popular form of document and is rarely used, only for minor changes in Will.

Drafting of a Will:

It is not necessary that any technical words or terms of art be used in a will, but only that the wording be such that the intention of the testator can be known therefrom.[21] Though there is no prescribed form of Will but it is imperative that the words used in the Will are clear and specific enough to ascertain the intention of the testator. Minor errors in the names or description can be ignored[22] but it is best to avoid the errors as far as possible. Errors in description or names may require the court to take evidence about the true intention but such procedures take more time. Persons with similar names may be referred along with their father's name and/or their relationships with the testator.

Blanks in a Will must definitely be avoided as even court can not supply the blanks and such portion of the Will shall be ignored as void.[23] See following *illustrations:*

(i) A man has an aunt, Caroline, and a cousin, Mary, and has no aunt of the name of Mary. By his will be bequeaths 1,000 rupees to "my aunt, Caroline" and 1,000 rupees to "my cousin, Mary" and afterwards bequeaths 2,000 rupees to "my before-mentioned aunt, Mary". There is no person to whom the description given in the will can apply, and evidence is not admissible to show who was meant by "my before-mentioned aunt, Mary". The bequest is therefore void for uncertainly.

(ii) '*A*', bequeaths 1,000......................leaving a blank for the name of the legatee. Evidence is not admissible to show what name the testator intended to insert.

(iii) '*A*', bequeaths to '*B*'......................rupees, or "my estate

---

21 Section 74 of Succession Act, 1925
22 Section 76 ibid.
23 Section 82 r/w s. 89 ibid.

of. Evidence is not admissible to show what sum or what estate the testator to insert.

Similarly a will or bequest not expressive of any definite intention is void for uncertainty.[24] See this *illustration*:

If a testator says "I bequeath goods to *A*" or "I bequeath to *A*" or "I leave to *A* all the goods mentioned in the Schedule" and no Schedule is found annexed to the Will, or "I bequeath 'money', 'wheat', 'oil' or the like", without saying how much, this is void.

Inconsistency and repetition can have very undesirable result. Where two clauses or gift in a will are irreconcilable, so that they cannot possibly stand together, the last shall prevail.[25] See these *illustrations:*

(i) The testator by the first clause of his will leaves his estate of Ramnagar "to *A*", and by the last clause of his leaves it "to *B* and not to *A*". *B* will have it.

(ii) If a testator at the commencement of his will gives his house to '*A*', and at the close of it directs that his house shall be sold and the proceeds invested for the benefit of '*B*', the latter disposition will prevail.

The logic of giving effect to latter clause is that within one Will it is the 'Last and Final' and therefore the enforceable Will. But this principle too has exceptions. Hence the best course is to avoid repetition.

The smallest Will which was given effect was on the back of a postage stamp and longest Will may run into hundred of hand written pages. It really does not matter. But use of stamp paper for writing the Will, unless explained, is not only unnecessary but is also suspicious. Use of clean unwritten blank paper is the only recommended medium. If videography is intended, it should be in

---

24   Section 89 ibid.
25   Section 88 ibid.

addition to the written Will.

As explained above the ordinary rule of thumb is that a will must avoid repetition. Either start with names of legatees and give specific property to each or start with each property, give its description and bequeath it to specific person or persons. Ensure that the list is not repeated as it may have undesirable consequences.

Details to be mentioned in the Will.

There is no statutory requirement of details to be mentioned except to avoid those errors pointed out in previous chapter and the manner of execution and attestation dealt with in next chapter. It is however prudent to incorporate certain details in a Will. These may be summarised as under:

1. Proper identification of testator with name, address and father's/husband's name. If there are more than one addresses, then prefix one address as a permanent address.

2. Proper identification of witnesses with name, address and father's/husband's name.

3, Proper identification of all the legatees (beneficiaries) with relationship and father's/husband's name and if possible brief address or at least the name of city if stationed out of town.

4. Proper identification of all the immovable properties like addresses, or landmarks, area and/or floors etc.

5. Proper identification of all the moveable properties like Bank names, bank account numbers, locker number, shares or holdings in certificates with consecutive numbers and name of company etc. Brevity may create problems.

6. A brief family history of testator and facts of marriage and children etc. If unmarried details of (living and dead) siblings and parents etc.

7. A brief reason for creating the Will (generally "life being uncertain") or for ousting a natural legal heir from

succession.

8. A statement that all properties are self acquired properties and are not co-parcenary (HUF), ancestral or joint properties.

9. Specific share if it pertains to a joint property.

10. Note that nominations made in the bank accounts etc. are of no legal effect unless ratified in the Will. Therefore do not omit to mention those nominations which need to affirmed.

Some of the details mentioned above are aimed at lending credence that the Will was drafted by the testator himself who alone had all the personal information about his/her affairs.

Execution or signing of Will.

In law, signing of a document, to formally give effect to the same, is called execution and the person signing the document is called executant. Therefore a testator is also an executant. The persons in whose presence a documents is executed (signed) are witnesses and these witnesses also sign the document as a mark of their having witnessed the execution. By attestation is meant to be the signing of a document to signify that the attester is a witness to the execution of the document.[26] Thus the act of signing as witness is called attestation.

Broadly there are following three rules about execution and attestation of Will:

1. The testator shall sign or shall affix his mark to the will, or it shall be singed by some other person in his presence and by his direction.[27]

2. The signature or mark of the testator, or the signature of the person signing for him, shall be so placed that it shall appear that it was intended thereby to give effect to the writing as a will.[28]

3. The will shall be attested by two or more witnesses, each of whom has seen the testator sign of affix his mark to the will or has seen some other person sign the will, in the presence and by the direction of the testator, or has received from the testator a personal acknowledgement of his signature or mark, or of the signature of such other

---

26   Beni Chand v. Kamala Kunwar, AIR 1977 SC 63.
27   S. 63(a) ibid.
28   S. 63(b) ibid.

person; and each of the witnesses shall sign the will in the presence of the testator but it shall not be necessary that more than one witness be present at the same time and no particular form of attestation shall be necessary.[29]

It cannot be presumed from the mere signatures of two persons appearing at the foot of the endorsement of registration of a Will that they had appended their signatures to the document as attesting witnesses nor can be construed to have done so in their capacity as attesting witness. Section 68, Evidence Act requires an attesting witness to be called as a witness to prove the due execution and attestation of the Will and this provision should be complied with in order that those two persons might be treated as attesting witness.[30]

It may, therefore be emphasised the attesting witness plays very important role not only in attestation but also in proving the due execution of Will when its authenticity is challenged. Non-availability of witness can have deleterious effect. Therefore witnesses must be carefully chosen with due emphasis on young age of witnesses who may not predecease the testator. Unless engaged in professional capacity, a complete stranger or a person from far off place should not be involved as witness as it shall arouse suspicion. Read more in the Chapter relating to 'Suspicious Circumstances'.

Advanced discussion:

(May skip to next chapter here)

Writing one's name, parentage and address in the opening part of

---

29   S. 63(c) ibid.
30   Mohinder v. Bugli Devi, 1993 (1) DMC 480 P&H (DB).

documents such as sale deed, gift deed, mortgage deed, lease deed, agreements, promissory notes and even Wills is customary in our country but invariably all these documents are signed by the executant and writing the name of the executant while describing his identity in the opening part of the document is not taken or treated as his signature in lieu of execution of that document.[31]

The fact whether a particular witness is an attesting witness or not depends upon the evidence given by that witness.[32]

In every case the Court must be satisfied that the names were written *animo attestendi*. Evidence is admissible to show whether the witness had the intention to attest. The attesting witness must subscribe with the intention that the subscription made should be complete attestation of the will, and the evidence is admissible to show whether such was the intention or not.[33]

The requirement is that attestation of Will must be made by two or more witnesses and not that the both must be present at the same time.[34]

A combined reading of section 68 of the Evidence Act and Section 63 of the Succession Act, 1925 would, therefore, require at least one attesting witness to be examined and the said witness should speak not only about the testator's signature or affixing his mark to the Will but also that each of the witnesses has signed the Will in the presence of the testator.[35]

When Testator, himself did not put his signatures, no question of attestation can arise. Attestation by witnesses before the executor

---

31 Leela Karwal v. J.D. Karwal, AIR 1986 All 220 (DB).
32 Girija Datt v. Gangotri Datt, AIR 1955 SC 346.
33 M. L. Abdul Jabbar Sahib v. M. V. Venkata Sastri, AIR 1969 SC 1147.
34 Karri Nookaraju v. Putra Venkatarao, AIR 1974 AP 13.
35 Illyas vs. Badshah alias Kamla, AIR 1990 MP 334: 1990 MP RCJ 477.

put his signature is not valid consequently the Will is also invalid.[36]

A Scribe (document writer) proving that the Will was written by him and duly read over to testator who thereafter read over the Will and after the testator signed the Will, the scribe along with other marginal witnesses signed the Will. Such scribe can be taken as an attesting witness.[37]

36 Virendra Singh Pal v. Kashibai, 1999 Civ. CR 130 MP (DB).
37 Dhyan Chand v. Savitri Devi, AIR 1998 HP 37 (DB).

Appointment of executor.

Executer is the person authorised by testator to fulfil his desires as expressed in Will, after the death of Testator. Executor is thus the administrator of the estate of deceased whose administration starts immediately upon the death of Testator. If executor has any problem in executing the Will, he may approach the court for Probate and such remedy as he may be entitled to.

The acts of representation of the testate of the deceased can be done only by the executor. That is why the probate shall be granted only to an executor: the grantee of the probate alone can sue or prosecute any suit or otherwise act as representative of the deceased and upon the death of one of several executors. The obligations to administer accrues to the surviving executors. Therefore it is of utmost importance that an executor may be carefully chosen. More than one executors can also be chosen to act together. Alternatively a series of executors can be appointed one of whom shall act and in case of a refusal, recusal or disability by one, the next executor shall perform.

The sanctity of the Will and, therefore, of the appointment of executor is highlighted by the law which declares that the probate shall be granted "only to an executor appointed by the Will".[38]

The ordinary method of appointing an executor for a testator is to nominate a person in the body of his Will by the express designation of executor. Even though a testator may fail to nominate a person on express terms to be his 'executor', yet if upon a reasonable construction of his Will it appears that a particular person has been appointed to perform the essential duties of the executor such an appointment is sufficient to

---

38   Rustam Ardeshir Gagrat; In re:, AIR 1990 Bom 111: 1989 Mah LJ 1034: (1989) 3 Bom CR 310.

constitute that person an executor.[39]

Advanced discussion:

(May skip to next chapter here)

Even if the term 'executor' is not expressly used in the Will but duty in nature of executor is assigned to a person, such person can be treated as executor of Will.[40] Where the testator did not nominate the plaintiffs in the Will by express word 'executor" yet he recommended and handed them the right to obtain the probate which right appertains only to an executor; it was held that the language clearly indicates the testator's intention that the plaintiffs should be the executors of his Will.[41]

The provisions of Section 213(1) of the Indian Succession Act that an executor or a legatee cannot establish his right as a legatee without obtaining probate of the Will in question but there is nothing to prevent the executor from dealing with the property of the deceased without obtaining probate because under section 211 of the Indian Succession Act, the executor is the legal representative of the deceased for all purposes and the property of the deceased vests in him and the grant of probate is not a condition precedent to such vesting of estates in the executor and or his acting as executor.[42]

If no executor can be ascertained from the Will, the letter of administration can be granted to the sole beneficiary under the Will.[43]

When no executor was appointed either expressly or by necessary

39   Jonnala Veerareddy v. Marreddy Seethomma, AIR 1976 AP 306 (DB): 1976 Andh LT 140.
40   Simanapalli Rama Rao v. G. Kamalamma, 1993 (2) DMC 246 AP: 1993 (2) CCC 70 AP.
41   Harish Chander Prasad v. Jagar Nath Prasad, AIR 1985 Pat 283 (DB): 1985 Pat LJR 918.
42   Gobinda Ballav Chakraborty v. Biswanath Mustafa, AIR 1980 Cal 143: (1979) 2 Cal LJ 325.
43   Inder Chand Nayyar v, Sarvadeshik Arya Pratinidhi Sabha, AIR 1977 Del 34: 1976 RLR 443.

implication, Probate cannot be granted but only letter of administration can be granted.[44]

If an executor starts functioning as an executor without obtaining probate and his actions are in derogation of the terms of the Will and prejudicial to the interest of the estate, the beneficiaries cannot remain helpless. They cannot assert their rights under the Will as legatees without probate of the Will, by filing a suit. In such a case the remedy available is to apply to the Court for removal of the executor.[45]

When no executor was appointed in the Will, the Universal or residuary legatee is entitled to letter of administration in respect of whole estate in exclusion to the other legatee.[46]

When no specific grounds have been included/enumerated in section 301[47] for removal of any private executor or administrator. The executor so named in the will, therefore, should be removed only when a proper case in that behalf is made out for last wishes of the deceased as expressed in his will nominating a person and an executor should be highly respected. While exercising power under Section 301 of the Indian Succession Act, the Court must guard itself against any frivolous attempt for collateral purposes to remove the executor. If the Court finds that the person making an application has not come out with a clear title or has not come with clean hands, the application should be refused.[48] There cannot be a deemed renunciation by executor.[49]

---

44 Soundararaja Peter v. Florance Chellaith, AIR 1975 Mad 194 (DB): (1975) 2 Mad LJ 164: 87 Mad LW 848.
45 F.C.S. Amalnathan v. J.S. Victor Basco, 1995 (1) DMC 468: AIR 1995 Kant 258.
46 Pari Hingorani v. Shakuntala, AIR 1987 Del 307.
47 Succession Act, 1925
48 Kusum Kurre v. Dharam Singh, 1986 (2) DMC 87 MP.
49 Samir Chandra Das v Bibhas Chandra Das,AIR 2010 SC 1962.

Registration of Will.

A Will is not compulsorily registerable. Therefore the registration is entirely optional. While registration may have a psychological effect of authenticity, it does not take away the proof of execution and attestation, discussed in previous chapters. Therefore if a Will is challenged, its due execution and attestation has to be proved by evidence. Registration may or may not be helpful in proving the execution and attestation, depending upon the evidence led in the case.

There is however one advantage with registration that a registered Will can not be lost, at least a copy thereof will remain with registrar who can issue a certified copy in accordance with rules to the legal heirs of a deceased testator.

Section 41(1) of the Indian Registration Act provides that : "A will..... presented for registration by the testator..... may be registered in the same manner as any other document. Section 41(2) provides that in the case of registration of a Will presented for registration by any other person entitled to present it shall be registered if the Registering Officer is satisfied (a) that the Will or authority was executed by the testator or donor as the case may be, (b) that the testator or donor is dead; and (c) that the person presenting the will or authority is, under Section 40, entitled to present the same. From Section 41 of the Indian Registration Act, it is clear that if a Will is sought to be registered by presenting it by the testator, it has to be registered in the same manner as any other document.

Registration of a Will though not required under law is only a piece of evidence of the execution. It cannot have greater sanctity. Registration cannot take the place of due attestation of the document as per the provisions of Section 63(c) of the Succession Act.[50]

Advanced discussion:

(May skip to next chapter here)

Where a testator admitted execution of the will before a Sub-Registrar and affixed his thumb impression, there was a proper execution of the will, apart from the question whether there was such proper execution before.[51]

Mere registration of a document, selectively a will is not sufficient in proof of its due execution, but the certificate endorsed by the registration officer on the document is admissible to prove that the executant was of sound mind.[52]But the certificate would not enable the court to presume animus at factum (combination of intention with the act) on the part of the executant.[53]

Registering Officer and the identifying witness before him can be treated as attesting witness of the Will if it is proved that they signed the Will in the presence of the testator after receiving from him an acknowledgment of his signature on the Will.[54]

A distinction has to be kept in mind in understanding the rigours of requirements of attestation and its proof. It is well settled that a document which compulsorily requires registration has to be completed before it is presented for registration, The position is different in the case of documents which are not compulsorily registerable. In such cases, it is enough for compliance with the

---

50 Karri Nookaraju v. Putra Venkatarao, AIR 1974 AP 13.
51 Theresa v. Francis, AIR 1921 Bom 156.
52 Venkata Rama Rao v. Bhaskararao, AIR 1962 AP 29.
53 Beepathumma v. Mohammed Nakoor Meera Rowther, AIR 1977 Ker 54.
54 Lal Singh v. Bant Singh, AIR 1983 P&H 384.

rules of execution and attestation if the executant actually admits the execution before the Sub Registrar and the identifying witnesses. It is possible to say that Will is not being compulsorily registerable, it is enough if the testator admits the execution before the Sub Registrar and the identifying witness.[55]

In a case where the document is a will which does not require registration, the Sub-Registrar and the identifying witnesses, if they conform to the law regarding attestation, may become attesting witnesses.[56]

Though the will must be attested by two or more witnesses but a Sub Registrar while registering a will presented to him by the testator can be regarded to be an attesting witness.[57]

A will is not required by law to be registered. Thus, it might be enough for the compliance of the rule of execution and attestation if the testator actually admits execution before the Sub-Registrar and the identifying witness. Like a mortgage deed a will need not be executed and attested first before it is presented for registration. Only two safeguards are needed for a will, namely, execution and attestation. If these are supplied at the registration, the requirements are fulfilled. The case of a will therefore is entirely different from a case of a mortgage and cannot be relied upon as a clear guide.[58]

---

55 K.M. Varghese v. K.M. Oommen, AIR 1994 Ker 85.
56 Punnakkal Konnu Ammu v. Thekkekara Kunhunni Krishnan, AIR 1965 Ker 32.
57 Makhan Mal L. Ram Ditta Mal v. Pritam Devi, AIR 1961 Punjab 411.
58 Lechman Singh v. Surendra Bahadur Singh, AIR 1932 All 527.

Will by physically challenged persons.

Every person of sound mind not being a minor may dispose of his property by will.[59] A married woman may dispose by will of any property which she could alienate by her own act during her life. Persons who are deaf or dumb or blind are not thereby incapacitated for making a will if they are able to know what they do by it. A person who is ordinarily insane may make a will during an interval in which he is of sound mind. But no person can make a will while he is in such a state of mind, whether arising from intoxication or from illness or from any other cause that he does know that what he is doing. See these *illustrations:*

> (i) A can perceive what is going on in his immediate neighbourhood, and can answer familiar question, but has not a competent understanding as to the nature of his property, or the persons who are of kindred to him, or in whose favour in would be proper that he should make his will. A cannot make valid will.

> (ii) A executes an instrument purporting to be his will, but he does not understand the nature of the instrument, nor the effect of its provisions. This instrument is not a valid will.

> (iii) A being very feeble and debilitated, but capable of exercising a judgement as to the proper mode of disposing of his property, makes a will. This is a valid will.

Therefore the person executing a Will must be able to identify the relatives/legatees as also the property to show sound disposition of mind.

The illustration (iii) above clearly demonstrate that the old age or feebleness due to illness by itself does not affect right to execute a Will.

---

59   Section 59 ibid.

Suspicious circumstances.

Will is a sacred instrument which is given effect after the death of its executant i.e. Testator. The court which hears the challenge to Wills (i.e. Probate Court) is called the court of conscience. While other documents are enforceable upon proof of its due execution, a Will is not only need to be attested, as explained in earlier chapter, it's execution must also be beyond suspicion. Any element or fact which makes execution of Will suspicious, may render the Will unenforceable or void.

The person relying upon or claiming under a Will apart from being a legatee is at first 'Propounder' of the Will. It is his duty not only to prove due execution and attestation of Will but also to explain suspicious circumstances, if any.

Since Will is a document which is brought to light after the testator's death, who does not remain available either to admit or deny the document or the statement made therein, and therefore, where the document of Will is shrouded with suspicion, the propounder is required to clear the suspicious circumstances, to the satisfaction of the Court's conscience not only about its execution, but more particularly about its authenticity also. The burden lies only on the person, who sets up the theory of Will to prove the due execution of Will and to remove the suspicious circumstances surrounding the document.[60]

Cases in which the execution of the will is surrounded by suspicious circumstances stand on a different footing. A shaky signature, a feeble mind, an unfair and unjust disposition of property, the propounder himself taking a leading part in the

---

60 Om Prakash Sharma v. Saraswatibai, AIR 1998 MP 226 (DB): 1998 (1) MP LJ 183: 1998 (2) Hindu LR 153.

making of the will under which he receives a substantial benefit and such other circumstances raise suspicion about the execution of the will. That suspicion cannot be removed by the mere assertion of the propounder that the will bears the signature of the testator or that the testator was in a sound and disposing state of mind and memory at the time when the will was made, or that those like the wife and children of the testator who would normally receive their due share in his estate were disinherited because the testator might have had his own reasons for excluding them. The presence of suspicious circumstances makes the initial onus heavier and therefore, in cases where the circumstances attendant upon the execution of the will excite the suspicion of the Court, the propounder must remove all legitimate suspicions before the document can be accepted as the last will of the testator. [61]

The Will is the will of the testator and he has, under the law, the freedom to give his property to whomsoever he likes. Therefore what strikes the Court as an eccentric or an unjust or an unnatural disposition can certainly be taken as a consideration on the main question of finding out whether the testator was acting as a free agent and with a sound disposing and understanding mind. But once it is established that the testator was free and had a sound disposing mind, it is no longer the duty of the Court to go further to inject its own ethics of what is or is not a moral or a fair disposition according to the Court's own standard.[62] Yet it is prudent to give brief reasons for every so called eccentric wishes incorporated in the Will.

Initial burden of proving the Will as a document is upon the

---

61   Jaswant Kaur v. Amrit Kaur, AIR 1977 SC 74: 1977(1) SCC 369: 1977(1) SCR 925: 1977 Hindu LR 731; See also Vrindavanibai Sambhaji Mane vs. Ramchandra Vithal Ganeshkar, AIR 1995 SC 2086
62   Chinmoyee Saha v. Debendra Lal Saha, AIR 1985 Cal 349 (DB): (1985) 89 Cal WN 832.

propounder but thereafter if any allegation of undue influence or fraud is made by the caveator, the burden is upon the caveator (challenger to will) whereafter the onus shift to propounder to remove the suspicious circumstances.[63]

Bequeath in favour of a person who looked after testatrix and maintain good relations with her while exclusion of others who did not look after her is not unnatural in a Will.[64]

---

63 Susama Bala Devi v. Anath Nath Tarafdar, AIR 1973 Cal 377 (DB).
64 Vrindavanibai Sambahji Mane vs. Ramchandra Vithal Ganeshkar, AIR 1995 SC 2086: 1995(5) SCC 215: 1995(4) Scale 271: 1995(7) JT 363; See also Misri Lal vs. Daulati Devi, 1997 (7) SCC 133: AIR 1997 SC 3819.

Nuncupative, Oral, Digital or Electronic Will.

A will has to be in writing. This can be inferred from the fact that mandatory requirement of execution (signing) by testator in presence of two witnesses is not possible. Since Information Technology Act, 2000 specifically exclude a will from its operation, a videography or a digitally signed electronic document can not be used as a Will.

Oral Wills were prevalent in Rome but were later abolished. Presently an nuncupative or oral will is unknown in law. The only exception is in this case is Muslim Law which permits oral will subject to certain conditions but that is beyond the scope of this work. Another exception is the privileged Wills permitted to armymen and marines etc. in some countries.

However an ordinary person can not execute a will in any manner other than writing on paper with due execution and attestation as explained above.

Joint and Mutual Will.

Joint Wills and Mutual Wills though appearing to be similar are not same. These are two different kinds of Wills in both of which there are more than one testator. The legal effect of both differ in respect of some crucial aspects. Such Wills are complex documents and an attempt to draft the same without professional help should be avoided. These types of documents are ordinarily executed by couples or close relatives with variety of common or overlapping interests.

Joint Will:

A joint Will, though for all apparent purposes, is a simple testamentary instrument, constitutes or unites in the testamentary disposition of two or more persons. The document only evidences that two or more persons have executed their Wills in a single document.

Mutual Will:

Mutual Wills as distinguished from joint are described as reciprocal Wills. Reciprocity in the matter of bequests under the Will is the sigil and signet of a mutual Will. The testators should confer upon each other reciprocal benefits.[65]

Advanced discussion:

(May skip to next chapter here)

A joint will is a will made by two or more testators contained in a

---

65   V. Sarada v. K.V. Narayana Menon, AIR 1989 Ker 155: 1987 Ker LJ 606.

single document, duly executed by each testator, disposing either of their separate properties, or of their joint property. It is not, however, recognised in the English law as a single will. It operates on the death of each testator as his will disposing of his own separate property, and is in effect two or more wills.[66]

Under a joint and mutual will, there is an implied understanding that after the death of one or more of the testators the other or others will not be entitled to revoke the will and they are bound by it. Such a revocation will be unauthorised and it will amount to a breach of truth towards the deceased testator or testators. The will then became irrevocable and the remaining testators alone by themselves could not revoke or change it. The surviving testators will then assume the role of trustees on behalf of the legatees and they will not be entitled to change the will of the deceased persons who could not express their desires on account of death.[67]

Where three Wills were executed by three testators in a single document, each Will has got its own identity and separates standings. So the Will in regard to the properties of insane person can be safely severed without causing any legal invalidity for the operation of the remaining part of the Will and the disposition of the properties of the other two testators.[68]

---

66   Kochu Govindan Kaimal v. Thayankoot Thekkot Lakshmi Amma, AIR 1959 SC 71: 1959 Ker LJ
      188: (1959) 1 Mad LJ SC 44: 1959 (1) Supp SCR 1,
67   George Mitran v. T.H. Gerfrude, 1990 (1) DMC 582 Ker.
68   V. Sarada v. K.V. Narayana Menon, AIR 1989 Ker 155: 1987 Ker LJ 606.

Effect of Multiple Wills.

A Will enforceable in law is the last desire of a person and drawn in writing and attested in accordance with the law. Therefore every Will executed by a testator automatically supersedes (or cancels) previous Will.

In case the latest Will, for any reason, is found to be invalid, the Will executed immediately prior to last will become valid and enforceable in law.

It is however strongly recommended that every Will must expressly cancel the previous Will. This shall not only avoid confusion but shall also explain the lingering suspicion which may arise due to existence of multiple Wills.

Beneficiaries or the legatees

A bequest by Will can be made in favour of any person living or juristic (e.g. a Corporation or Trust). Bequest can also be made so as to create a new juristic entity like a Trust. Unlike other transfers, there is no restriction in respect of bequest being made in favour of minor, lunatic or insolvent persons etc. There is no requirement that the heirs should make any gesture of formal acceptance of Will during the lifetime of Testator. The Will operates with it's own force.

Bequest to Religious or Charitable purpose:

Law prohibit last moment change of heart to donate the properties to religion or charity. It is provided that no person having a nephew or niece or any nearer relative shall have power to bequest any property to religious or charitable uses, except by a will executed not less than twelve month before his death, and deposited within six months from its execution in some place provided by law for the safe custody of the wills of living persons.[69]

Therefore any bequest made within 12 months preceding the death, shall be unenforceable. See this *illustration:*

> 'A' having a nephew makes a bequest by a will not executed and deposited as required—
>> for the relief poor people'
>> for the maintenance of sick soldiers;
>> for erection or support of a hospital;
>> for the education and preferment of orphans;
>> for the support of scholars;

---

69   Section 118 ibid.

for the erection or support of a school;
for the building and repairs of a bridge;
for the making of roads;
for the erection or support of a church;
for the repairs of a church;
for the benefit of ministers of religion;
for the formation or support of a public garden.

In case of death of testator within 12 months from the date or execution of Will, all the above bequests are void.

Unborn person

No bequest can be invalid by reason only that any person for whose benefit it may have been made was not born at the date of the testator's death. This rule, however, is subject to the limitations and provisions contained in Sections 113, 114, 115 and 116 of the Indian Succession Act, 1925.[70] If a person answering the description given by testator is alive at the death of the testator, or comes into existence between that event and such later time the property shall, at such later time, go to that person, or, if he is dead, to his representatives. See these *Illustrations:*

(*i*) *A* bequeaths 1,000 rupees to the eldest son of *B*. At the death of the testator, *B* has no son. The bequest is void.

(*ii*) *A* bequeaths 1,000 rupees to *B* for life, and after his death to the eldest son of *C*. At the death of the testator, *C* had no son. Afterwards, during the life of *B*, a son is born to *C*. Upon *B*'s death the legacy goes to *C*'s son.

(*iii*) *A* bequeaths 1,000 rupees to *B* for life, and after his death to the eldest son of *C*. At the death of the testator, *C* had no son. Afterwards, during the life of *B*, a son named *D* is born to

---

70 Raman Nadar Viswanathan Nadar v. Snehappoo Rasalamma, AIR 1970 SC 1759: 1970 (2) SCJ 738: 1969(3) SCC 42: 1970(2) SCR 471.

C, *D* dies, then *B* dies. The legacy goes to the representative of *D*.

(*iv*) *A* bequeaths his estate of Green Acre to *B* for life, and at his deceased, to the eldest son of *C*. Up to the death of *B*, *C* has had no son. The bequest to *C*'s eldest son in void.

(*v*) *A* bequeaths 1,000 rupees to the eldest son of *C*, to be paid to him after the death of *B*. At the death of the testator *C* has no son; but a son is afterwards born to him during the life of *B* and is alive at *B*'s death. *C*'s son is entitled to the 1,000 rupees.

Therefore the legacy in favour of unborn person is dependent upon the birth of such person, in the absence of which the bequest is void.

Effect of death of legatee

By virtue of Section 119 of Succession Act, 1925, in a case where bequest is not entitled to immediate possession of the thing bequeathed, the right to receive it at the proper time becomes vested in the legatee on the testator's death and in the event of the death of the legatee without having received the legacy the said right to receive it passes to the legal representatives of the legatee. This is, however, subject to a contrary intention being expressed in the Will.[71]

Incomplete adoption:

If the testator regarded a person as his adopted son and described him as such in the will, the Will cannot be regarded to have contained a false statement and as such to be a suspicious document event if it is shown that the alleged adoption was not

---

71   Usha Subbarao v. B.N. Vishveswaraiah, 1996 (5) SCC 201: AIR 1996 SC 2260.

legal and complete being unaccompanied by requisite formal ceremonies. That apart assuming that the propounder was not the adopted son of the testator, a mistaken statement made by the testator in the will as to the status of the legatee cannot operate to the prejudice of the legatee and cannot be regarded to be suspicious circumstances to throw doubt on the genuineness of the Will.[72]

---

72   Sonam Topgyal Bhutia v. Gompu Bhutia, AIR 1980 Sikkam 33 (DB).

Rule against perpetuity.

Title of property is a serious matter for the Government as well as State. Doubts about title of property often has serious effect on the affairs of State. For example, if it is not known, who is owner, how a property can be acquired or requisitioned in case of War or calamity. Apart from war, the title of property is also important from the point of view of economy. A property without title can not be mortgaged and thus remain unproductive. A property mortgaged to obtain loan so that a new factory may be established not only is good for the Government for taxes but also good for economy as it creates jobs. Further if there is no rightful owner of property, it belongs to the State (called escheat).

For these reasons there is a principle of law called 'Rule against Perpetuity'. It prevents a person from placing such qualifications and criteria in the Will that will continue to control or affect the distribution of assets long after Testator has died, a concept often referred to as control by the "dead hand". While ordinary rule in England is that the transmission of title of property must be completed within 21 years from the death of testator, the problem is little more complex in India. See this provision:

> "No bequest is valid where by vesting of the thing bequeathed may be delayed beyond the lifetime of one of more persons living at the testator's death and the majority of some person who shall be in existence at the expiration of that period, and to whom, if he attains full age, the thing bequeathed is to belong."

If it seems obscure, do not worry. Legal jargon is always obscure. Now read these Illustrations:

(*i*) *A* fund is bequeathed to *A* for his life and after his death to *B* for his life; and after *B*'s death to such of the sons of *B* as shall first attain the age of 25. *A* and *B* survive the testator. Here the son of *B* who shall first attain the age of 25 may be a son born after the death of the testator; such son may not attain 25 until more than 18 years have elapsed from the death of the longer liver at *A* and *B*; and the vesting of the fund may thus be delayed beyond the lifetime of *A* and *B* and the minority of the sons of *B*. The bequest after *B*'s death is void.

(*ii*) *A* fund is bequeathed to *A* for his life, and after his death to *B* for his life, and after *B*'s death to such of *B*'s sons as shall first attain the age of 25. *B* dies in the lifetime of the testator, leaving one or more sons. In this case the sons of *B* are persons living at the time of the testator's decease, and the time when either of them will attain 25 necessarily falls within his own lifetime. The bequest is valid.

(*iii*) A fund is bequeathed to *A* for his life, and after his death to *B* for his life, with a direction that after *B*'s death it shall be divided among such of *B*'s children as shall attain the age of 18, but if no child of *B* shall attain that age, fund shall go to *C*. Here, the time for the division of the fund must arrive at the latest at the latest at the expiration of 18 years from the death of *B*, a person living at the testator's decease. All the bequests are valid.

(*iv*) A fund is bequeathed to trustees for the benefit of the testator's daughters, with a direction that, if any of them marry under age, her share of the fund shall be settled so as to devolve after her death upon such of her children as shall attain the age of 18. Any daughter of the testator to whom the directions applies must be in existence at his decease, and any portion of the fund which may eventually be settled as directed must vest not latter than 18 years from the death of the daughters whose share it was. All these provisions are valid.

Putting the above obscure jargon in simple words it can be said that a Will can create one life interest and thereafter one 'final' or complete bequest but the second bequest must be complete by the time second person attains age of 18 years. The last illustration aptly explain it.

Another way to look at the principle is that creation of successive life estates that too in favour of persons not in existence is not permissible in law and the life estate so created in favour of persons in existence and those not in existence would take effect with reference to those in existence at the time of the death of the testator and invalid as to the rest.[73]

A person cannot alter the line of succession allowed by law for the purpose of carrying out his own wishes and policy. A Will cannot create a course of succession unknown to Hindu Law. When successive estates are conferred, the inheritance must be such as is known to Hindu Law. It is on this basis that the Wills and gifts which direct an estate to go in an order of succession which excludes female heirs, that is, an estate in tail male, have been held to be invalid to that extent.[74]

73   G. Narayanan v. R.N. Rayagopalam, AIR 1987 Mad 75: (1987) 100 Mad LW 25.
74   Kashiram v. Bhura,AIR 1981 MP 236 DB: 1981 MPLJ 181: 1981 Jab LJ136.

NOTES

Proforma Wills

How to make a Will

NOTES

1. Specimen Will in favour of wife as life interest and subsequently to son disinheriting daughter.

WILL

I, _____ s/o Late _____ r/o _____,
New City,. make this my last and final WILL which shall be effective after my death and carried out to its terms.

WHEREAS I had executed a Will on _____ which was also registered with the office of Registrar, New City. I hereby revoke all previous wills including the aforesaid Will which may have been made by me at any time hereto before and declare this to be my last and final Will.

AND WHEREAS I AM MARRIED TO _____ for last 50 years and from this marriage I have one son namely _____ who is married to _____ and one daughter namely _____ who is married to _____.

AND WHEREAS I am the sole and absolute owner of the house/property No._____, New City by virtue of registered conveyance deed dated _____ executed in my favour .

AND WHEREAS I also have accounts with Bank/Post Office, fixed deposits, shares, and other moveable assets, jewellery etc., details of which are given in Schedule I below.

AND WHEREAS I had married my aforesaid daughter _____ and had made sufficient endowment and gifts to her for her settlement in life and who is happily married to _____ and does not need any more help from me

AND WHEREAS I have completed my 80th birthday and being in advanced age I intend to settle my affairs.

AND THEREFORE while cancelling my previous WILLS , I hereby make my last and final WILL in following terms:

1.   I hereby appoint my nephew _____ as an executor of this Will.

2.   I hereby accordingly leave, bequeath and give the my aforesaid property i.e. _____, New City, including the terrace and the floors there above which may come up hereafter alongwith the common areas and amenities to my

wife _____ with full liberty as its owner to enjoy the same but shall not be entitled to sell transfer or assign, gift or part with its possession;

3.   After the death of my wife the aforesaid property shall devolve   upon my son _____,with full with full liberty as its owner to sell, transfer, gift, mortgage or otherwise alienate the same in the manner he so pleases.

4.   God forbid, in the event my son Ashok predeceases me or my wife, the aforesaid property shall devolve upon my daughter in law _____ w/o _____ with full with full liberty as its owner to sell, transfer, gift, mortgage or otherwise alienate the same in the manner he so pleases.

5.   I bequeath all my remaining assets including other moveable assets described in Schedule I, to my wife _____ who shall be its absolute owner to enjoy the same in the manner she may pleases.

6.   Any asset not included above or which may be acquired by me after the execution of this will shall devolve upon my wife _____ who shall be its absolute owner to enjoy the

same in the manner she may pleases.

7.   It is hereby made clear that except the aforesaid beneficiaries, no other person shall be entitled to claim any right title or interest in any or my properties after my death.

In the presence of following witnesses, who have also signed in my presence, I the above name testator have hereunto set and subscribe my hand and signature on this ___ day of _____2014.

(_____)

Testator

Signed by the within named testator as his last will and testament in our presence, all being present at the same time. Thereafter at his request and in his presence and in the presence of one another we subscribed our respective names.

Witnesses :

1.

2.

Affirmed that aforesaid persons signed in my presence and in presence of one another.

(_____)

Testator

Place, Date and time:

Schedule I

1. Bank account No. _____ with _____ Bank, _____ Branch.

2. Share Certificate with consecutive no. _____ to _____ in respect of _____ shares in _____ Ltd.

3. Post Office account No. _____ with _____ Post office.

4. National Saving Certificate No. _____ for Rs. _____

5. Household Furniture and Fixtures, Utensils & Personal belongings

2. Specimen Will in respect of shareholding in a private company bequeathed to non-relative.

WILL

THIS IS THE last WILL and testament of me, _____ son of _____ resident of _____, New City. I hereby revoke all wills by me at any time hereto before made and declare this to be my last will in respect of my property covered by this Will. This will be effective after my death and carried out to its terms.

WHEREAS I am the sole owner of the 1,05,000 Equity shares (face value of Rs 10/- each) in the company _____ PVT. LTD having its registered office at _____ by virtue of share transferred in my favour dt _____ and presently covered by Folio No. _____ and Share Certificate No. _____ issued by the said Company from various other companies and persons and the same having been duly transferred in my favour without any protest or objection from any other quarter.

And whereas ABC and XYZ are our family friends known for their astute business acumen and have always stood by meat the time of our need.

(1) I hereby appoint XYX son of _____ R/O _____, New City to be sole executor of my

this will and the trustee of my above estate mentioned hereafter.

(2) I direct that my said executor shall so soon as convenient, shall obtain probate of this will and until that time administer the estate covered by Will till it is vested in accordance with my bequest.

(3) I know ABC for quite long time as I am having personal relations with him and in the best interests of the company I hereby bequeath him the above said shareholding in the said company and my other legal heirs shall have no right to interfere in the management of the said company.

(4) I accordingly leave, bequeath and give my aforesaid property i.e. above share holding with full liberty as its owner to enjoy, mange, sell, transfer or otherwise alienate the same in the manner as it pleases to ABC son of _____.

(5) Subject to above specific legacy I shall bequeath the rest and residue of my estate, moveable and immovable property including future assets by way of a separate will or codicils as the case may be which shall have no effect on this will which is last and final in respect of aforesaid property.

In witness whereof, I the above name testator have hereunto set and subscribe my hand and signature on this _____ day of _____2014.

(_____)
Testator

Signed by the within named testator as his last will and testament in our presence all being present at the same time. Thereafter at his request and in his presence and in the presence of one another we subscribed our respective names.

Witnesses :

1._____

_____

_____

2._____

_____

_____

(_____)

Testator

3. Will in respect of membership in Co-operative Housing society

Will

I, _____ w/o

_____ resident of

_____, New City

hereby make this my last and final WILL which shall be effective after my death and carried out to its terms.

WHEREAS I had executed a Will on _____ which was also registered with the office of Registrar, New City as document no. _____ which stands superseded by the present will.

AND WHEREAS after execution of the aforesaid Will dated _____ there have been changes in the circumstances like closure of bank accounts, disposal of assets due to personal requirements etc. Hence this fresh Will in respect of remaining assets.

AND WHEREAS I was working as a Accountant in ABC Corporation Ltd. till I superannuated in the year _____.

AND WHEREAS during my tenure the employees of ABC Corporation Ltd. had formed a society named ABCL Co-operative Group Housing Society Ltd. of which I am a registered member under Share Certificate No. _____ dated

_____.

AND WHEREAS I am not keeping good health due to old age and other ailments

THEREFORE this is last and final will is being executed by me which has been drafted on my instructions and executed in sound disposition of mind.

1. THAT I am married to _____ and I am blessed with four daughters from this wedlock namely

    1) _____   married   to

    _____.

    2) _____ married to _____.

    3) _____ married to _____.

    4) _____ married to _____.

They are all prosperous and well settled in their married life and do not require any further assistance from me.

2. That after may death, I do hereby bequeath, give, transmit, assign and transfer all my rights, title and interest as a member of aforesaid ABCL Co-operative Group Housing Society Ltd. to my husband _____ who shall be entitled to derive all benefits which may be available at that time to the members of the said society, without any objection, demur or hesitation on the part of any person, organization of my any other legal heir including the right to sell transfer or assign said membership in any manner as he may deem fit.

3. I bequeath all my remaining assets including other moveable assets, jewellery and household goods to my said husband _____ who shall be its absolute owner to enjoy the same in the manner he may pleases.

4.   Any asset not included above or which may be acquired by me after the execution of this will shall devolve upon my husband _____ who shall be its absolute owner to enjoy the same in the manner he may pleases.

6.   It is hereby made clear that except the aforesaid

beneficiaries, no other person shall be entitled to claim any right title or interest in any or my properties after my death.

In the presence of following witnesses, who have also signed in my presence, I the above name testator have hereunto set and subscribe my hand and signature on this ___ day of _____ 2014.

(_____)

Testator

Signed by the within named testator as his last will and testament in our presence, all being present at the same time. Thereafter at his request and in his presence and in the presence of one another we subscribed our respective names.

Witnesses :

1.

2.

Affirmed that aforesaid persons signed in my presence and in presence of one another.

(_____)

Testator

4. A sample of Codicil

Codicil

I, ABC son/daughter of _____ resident of _____New City, make this Codicil in addition to the Will made by me on 1st December 2012

1. By this Codicil I change the provisions of the said Will as follows:

2. I direct my Executors to pay a sum of Rs. 6,550/- to Mr. John Meyer in satisfaction of moneys borrowed by me, if not already repaid by me.

3. That in paragraph 8 of my Will, I hereby substitute the name of the Company 'Reliance Chemicals Ltd.' with the name 'Reliance Power Ltd.' which shall now be so read.

4. That all other respects the provisions contained in my Will dated 1st December 2011 will remain in full force and effect.

In the presence of following witnesses, who have also signed in my presence, I the above name testator have hereunto set and subscribe my hand and signature on this ___ day of _____ 2014.

(_____)

Testator

Signed by the within named testator as his last will and testament in our presence, all being present at the same time. Thereafter at his request and in his presence and in the presence of one another we subscribed our respective names.

Witnesses :

1. _____

2. _____

Affirmed that aforesaid persons signed in my presence and in presence of one another.

(_____)

Testator

5. Will in favour of minor with appointment of executor cum guardian.

WILL

I, _____ s/o Late _____ r/o _____, New City, do hereby revoke my all previous Wills and Codicils and make this my last and final WILL which shall be effective after my death and carried out to its terms.

WHEREAS I was married to _____ about 12 years back and from this marriage I have one son namely _____ who is presently a minor;

AND WHEREAS my wife left for heavenly abode last year leaving behind me and our only child named above;

AND WHEREAS I am the sole and absolute owner of the house/property No._____, New City by virtue of registered conveyance deed dated _____ executed in my favour .

AND WHEREAS I also have accounts with Bank/Post Office, fixed deposits, shares, and other moveable assets, jewellery etc., details of which are given in Schedule I below.

AND WHEREAS life being uncertain, I intend to settle my affairs.

AND THEREFORE while cancelling my previous WILLS and codicils, I hereby make this my last and final WILL in following terms:

1. I hereby appoint my nephew _____ as an executor of this Will who shall also act as guardian of my son _____ and administer the estate till my son attains the age of 25 years.

2. I hereby accordingly leave, bequeath and give the my aforesaid property i.e. _____, New City, including the terrace and the floors there above which may come up hereafter along with the common areas and amenities to aforesaid son _____ with full liberty as its owner to enjoy the same but shall not be entitled to sell transfer or assign, gift or part with its possession till the age of 30;

3. I also bequeath all my remaining assets including other moveable assets described in Schedule I, to my minor son _____ who shall be its absolute owner to enjoy the

same in the manner she may pleases.

4. God forbid, in the event my aforesaid son _____ predeceases me the aforesaid immoveable and moveable property shall devolve upon my sister in law _____ w/o _____ with full with full liberty as its owner to sell, transfer, gift, mortgage or otherwise alienate the same in the manner she so pleases.

5. I hereby bequeath my automobile with registration No. _____ to my niece _____ daughter of _____ who shall be entitled to take immediate possession of the vehicle and shall have full liberty as its owner to sell, transfer, gift, mortgage or otherwise alienate the same in the manner she so pleases.

6. Any asset not included above or which may be acquired by me after the execution of this will shall devolve upon my niece _____ who shall be its absolute owner to enjoy the same in the manner she may pleases.

In the presence of following witnesses, who have also signed in my presence, I the above name testator have hereunto set and subscribe my hand and signature on this ___ day of _____ 2014.

(_____)

Testator

Signed by the within named testator as his last will and testament in our presence, all being present at the same time. Thereafter at his request and in his presence and in the presence of one another we subscribed our respective names.

Witnesses :

1.

2.

Affirmed that aforesaid persons signed in my presence and in presence of one another.

(_____)

Testator

Schedule I

1. Bank account No. _____ with _____ Bank, _____ Branch.

2. Share Certificate with consecutive no. _____ to _____ in respect of _____ shares in _____ Ltd.

3. Post Office account No. _____ with _____ Post office.

4. National Saving Certificate No. _____ for Rs. _____

5. Household Furniture and Fixtures, Utensils & Personal belongings

Certificate of Doctor

I have examined Mr _____ on the date of this will and wish to state that he appears to be in of sound mind and sound mental health at the time of making the above will.

Signature of doctor with seal. _____

{Note: The effect of clause 4 may be noted. This clause operates only if the son dies before his father. In case the minor dies after he had inherited the estate under Will, the property in his hand shall be governed by law of succession and not by this Will.}

6. A specimen of complex Will with provision for creating a Trust

WILL

I, _____ s/o Late _____ r/o _____, New City, do hereby revoke my all previous Wills and Codicils and make this my last and final WILL which shall be effective after my death and carried out to its terms.

WHEREAS I was married to _____ for about 30 years and from this marriage I have two sons and one daughter;

AND WHEREAS my wife left for heavenly abode last year leaving behind me and our aforesaid children;

AND WHEREAS I am the sole and absolute owner of the house/property No._____, New City by virtue of registered conveyance deed dated _____ executed in my favour .

AND WHEREAS I also have accounts with Bank/Post Office, fixed deposits, shares, and other moveable assets, jewellery etc., details of which are given in Schedule I below.

AND WHEREAS life being uncertain, I intend to settle my affairs.

AND THEREFORE while cancelling my previous WILLS and codicils, I hereby make this my last and final WILL in following terms:

1. I appoint XYZ to be the Executor of this my Will. In case he shall not be willing to act as an executor ABC or DEF respectively shall act as executor of this Will.

2. I direct my Executor to spend a sum not exceeding Rs. 5,000/- for funeral expenses and other obsequial ceremonies and no more. They shall not be liable to render any accounts in respect of any amounts so spent by them.

3. I direct my executor to collect my estate and pay all my just and legal debts, if any, due and owing by me to anyone.

5. I also direct my Executor to administer my estate and obtain Probate if necessary and also to pay and incur necessary costs, charges and expenses in relation to the collection of my Estate as well as for obtaining Probate and for any other necessary or incidental charges.

Specific bequests:

6. I hereby bequeath to my eldest son _____ the platinum engagement ring presented to me by my wife on my engagement with her.

7. I give to my daughter _____ all my shareholding in Reliance Chemical Co. Ltd.

8. I give to my second son _____

9. I give to my niece _____ the entire sum of Rs.100,000/- or more as the case may be lying in my Bank account No. 123, Bank of India, Main Branch, New City.

General Bequests:

10. I direct my Executors to give to my niece _____ at the time of her marriage a gift of gold worth Rs. 100,000/-.

11. I direct my Executors to give to my servant _____ who has served me loyally for 15 years a sum of Rs. 20,000/-.

General Bequests out of a Specific fund:

12.I direct my Executors to sell my flat in which I am living at the time of my death and its address is _____and use the net sale proceeds for payment of a sum of Rs. 300,000/- each to my eldest son _____ and my daughter_____ . Should either of them be not living, my Executors are directed to pay the share coming to such deceased child to his/her male children in equal shares. If both of them should die without leaving any male issue, then their share shall pass to the my second son namely_____.

Bequest to Charity:

13. I direct my Executors that out of the balance sale proceeds of my flat, they should pay a sum of Rs. 5,00,000/- to a charitable organization constituted for welfare of Helpage India or an organisation engaged in the welfare of aged people

Creation of Trust: (Implied Trust)

14. I further direct my Executor that out of the sale proceeds of my said flat after making payments as stated above, they should invest a sum of Rs. 1,000,000/- in Government Bank and utilize the income thereof for payment of such sums of money as they in

their discretion may consider fit from time to time by way of Annual Scholarships to meritorious students post graduate studies in the field of medicine.

Directions to Create a Trust:

15. I further direct my Executors that after making payments as stated above, they should liquidate all other assets and utilize the balance amount the purposes of creating a permanent Trust in the memory of my beloved Mother for research in the field of Medicine especially in respect of arthritis. This Trust shall be called "Jane Doe Foundation" which shall have two trustees to be nominated by the executor. The executor shall be free to nominate himself as trustee. The trustees will have the power to appoint their successors and the discretion to fix the amount of grant to be given to individuals or institutions every year for the promotion of the objects of the trust The trustees will also have the discretion to invest excess income of the Trust for the purposes of promoting the objects of the Trust.

Residuary Clause:

16. I direct the rest and residue of my estate whatever the same and wherever the same may be found to be equally distributed amongst the children (male and female) of niece_____ and nephew.

In the presence of following witnesses, who have also signed in my presence, I the above name testator have hereunto set and subscribe my hand and signature on this ___ day of _____ 2014.

(_____)

Testator

Signed by the within named testator as his last will and testament in our presence, all being present at the same time. Thereafter at his request and in his presence and in the presence of one another we subscribed our respective names.

Witnesses :

1.

2.

Affirmed that aforesaid persons signed in my presence and in presence of one another.

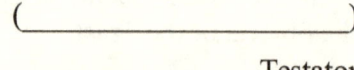

Testator

{Note 1: The residuary clause 16 is meaningless as the all remaining assets are part of the trust created under clause 15 itself. It is also an example of superfluous or defective drafting.}

{Note 2: The implied trust created under clause 14 and a the trust created under clause 15 are only for the purpose of example and should not be used together. Use only one of these clauses}

~.~.~

About the Author:

Sandeep Bhalla is a practicing lawyer domiciled in New Delhi, India. For past over two decades, he has written many books for the benefit of legal community. This book is one of the books aimed at students and common people interested in understanding the relevant law while also going into a mild debate that is required from a Legal Commentary.

Relating to author:

The author maintains his person blog at http//:sandeepbhalla.com.

His legal scrape-book is called 'http://lawmystery.com/'

Other Works of author:

1. Law of Maintenance

2. Law of obscenity in India

3. Commentary on Advocates Act, 1962

4. Commentary on Information Technology Act, 2000

5. Law of Joint property and its Partition

6. Company Law in India

and many more books.

~~~~~

www.ingramcontent.com/pod-product-compliance
Lightning Source LLC
Chambersburg PA
CBHW021413170526
45164CB00002B/629